The UNITED STATES MARINE BAND

ITS HISTORY
AND
ACHIEVEMENTS

A MESSAGE
FOR
MUSICIANS

United States Marine Corps
Recruiting Bureau
1100 South Broad Street
Philadelphia, Pa.

MAJOR GENERAL JOHN H. RUSSELL
COMMANDANT
UNITED STATES MARINE CORPS

THE UNITED STATES MARINE BAND

HISTORY *of the* MARINE BAND

S HORTLY after November 10, 1775, when Continental Congress said "Let there be Marines!" the citizens of Philadelphia saw on the drums of the Marines recruiting the regiment authorized, a rattlesnake, and under it the motto, Don't Tread on Me! That motto survives today on the drums of our Marine Corps and those drummers and fifers were the forerunners of the famous United States Marine Band.

Fifes and drums were the only musical instruments used by our military in the Revolution. A group of ten or more of them was called a "Band," and those gallant Marines possessed as fine a "Band" as any other military organization of the period. With the end of the Revolution came the end of everything military in our country and it is not until 1797 that we again find Marines and "Musics"—those that served on the frigates of the New Navy which Congress authorized in 1794.

In 1798 Congress decided that the Country could no longer get along without an organization of Marines and on July 11 of that year John Adams approved a bill that brought the New Marine Corps into being. This Act of Congress authorized a Drum Major, a Fife Major, and thirty-two "drums and fifes."

Some of these "Musics" were sent out on recruiting duty; some fell in battle on board our warships from 1798 to 1801 in the French Naval War; while a sufficient number were retained in Philadelphia and under Drum Major William Farr a military band of Marines was formed.

The first Headquarters of the Corps was under canvas, a short distance from the

TAYLOR BRANSON, LEADER

heart of the City of Philadelphia, which at that time was the capital of the United States.

The Marine Band often charmed Philadelphians with its splendid music.

The Headquarters remained in Philadelphia no longer than that city was continued as the Capital City. The last incident of importance participated in by the Marines in Philadelphia was the celebration of the Fourth of July in the year 1800. The Philadelphia *Universal Gazette* of July 10th, in describing this celebration, stated that "the Society of the Cincinnati distinguished the occasion by an elegant entertainment given at the City Tavern; at which the following toasts were given, to the animating notes of martial music, by the band belonging to Colonel Burrows's corps of Marines." This affair was made notable, as far as the Marines were concerned, by the Society of the Cincinnati conferring honorary membership upon Lieutenant-Colonel Commandant William Ward Burrows. It is on this occasion, also, that we read in the press for the first time of the famous United States Marine Band playing in public.

The National Capital moved from Philadelphia to Washington in 1800 and the Marines, already distinguished as "Presidential Troops," arrived in the Federal City in July of that year. Stopping for a few days in Georgetown, they pitched their tents on a most "beautiful hill overlooking the Potomac"—the same hill on which today is located the Naval Hospital.

The regard that Lieutenant-Colonel Burrows had for his Band is shown by his having it accompany him personally to Washington when he left Philadelphia for that city on July 12, 1800 to establish permanent headquarters in the new capital.

The Marine Band, with its inspiring music, did much to drive the gloom from the dismal Federal City, for Washington in those ancient days is described as the "City of Magnificent Distances," the "Wilderness City," the "Mud Hole," the "Capital of Miserable Huts," and the "City of Streets Without Houses."

One of the first public diversions furnished Washingtonians was the Marine Band concerts that took place on the hill, already mentioned, where the Marines had their camp. This hill was part of "the reservation selected for the

National University on E Street, between 23rd and 25th Streets." We read in Mrs. Thornton's Diary that during the latter part of August, 1800, she and her mother "went to the Hill to hear the Band," which was playing at the Marines' Camp on the "ground intended for the University." Encouraged by President John Adams, by Vice-President Thomas Jefferson and by Benjamin Stoddert, the first Secretary of the Navy, Colonel Burrows further developed the Band. After the arrival of Thomas Jefferson in Washington late in November, he and Colonel Burrows frequently were seen riding along the wooded bridle paths tracing the romantic Rock Creek discussing, among other things, the Marine Band.

The first recorded open air concert by the Marine Band in the Capital City was an informal one on August 21, 1800, when Washingtonians thronged the Marine Camp "on the Hill" to hear the Band led by William Farr, its first leader. There is no record of what instruments were played by the Band on this date but by December they consisted of two oboes, two clarinets, two French horns, a bassoon and a drum. Efforts to secure a bass drum were not successful for several months.

The Marine Band is the most ancient of American military bands and it was the only band of a public nature in Washington up to some time later than 1830.

After holding informal concerts at their camp and playing dance music for balls of the Washington Assembly —the first of which was held at Stelle's Hotel late in 1800 —the Band is said to have made its official debut when President Adams received at the White House on New Year Day, 1801.

This was the first of a long line of New Year Days, extending down to the present time, on which the band has played at White House receptions.

A. S. WITCOMB, 2nd LEADER

Since Jefferson's day it has played at every inauguration when that ceremony called for the presence of a Band. During its history every President has called upon it to play for functions at the White House and all have praised its efforts; but of its many friends the "Lady of the White House" always has been its warmest admirer and most helpful patron.

Short, scarlet coatees, faced and edged with blue and gold, with high blue collar edged with gold and blue shoulder straps ending in blue wings edged with gold, long blue scarlet-striped pantaloons, brown round hat, turned up on the left side with black leather cockade, formed the uniform of the Band at its formal debut. Each musician wore the black leather stock which gave to the Marines their historic sobriquet of *Leathernecks*.

Nowadays the uniforms usually prescribed for the Marine Band are special full dress, full dress, and blue undress. Special full dress and full dress are prescribed for state and other special occasions, the former being worn when the Band performs as an orchestra. The full dress and special full dress coats are of scarlet, in the tradition of the scarlet coats prescribed for ratings such as drum major and musician in Marine Corps uniform orders and regulations extending far back into the past century—to 1835, at least. For the leader, a blue coat is worn with both uniforms, a single coat having been adopted in 1916 in lieu of a scarlet special full dress and blue full dress coat. A blue cap for the leader and a scarlet cap for other members are the prescribed headgear, a white cap being alternate headgear with full dress for bandsmen.

The full dress coat bears ornamentation across the front, and aiguillettes and shoulder knots are worn therewith, except by the drum major, who has a white baldrick slung from his right shoulder across the body. The special full dress coat is devoid of these features. Special full dress is not worn by the drum major. With certain distinctions, blue undress is similar to that worn by corresponding ranks in the Marine Corps.

From 1798 to 1931 there have been seventeen leaders of the Marine Band. The exact date when Drum Major William Farr first entered the Marine Corps is not known at present, but the date given below is the earliest that has been located so far. The names, and periods of time served, of the various leaders of the Marine Band are as follows:

William Farr .... Jan. 21, 1799 to Nov. 22, 1804.
Charles S. Ashworth ...... Nov. 24, 1804 to Oct. 16, 1816.
Venerando Pulizzi .... Oct. 17, 1816 to Dec. 9, 1816.
John Powley .... Dec. 10, 1816 to Feb. 18, 1818.
Venerando Pulizzi .... Feb. 19, 1818 to July 13, 1824.
Venerando Pulizzi .... July 14, 1824 to Sept. 3, 1827.
John B. Cuvillier .... Sept. 3, 1827 to June 16, 1829.
Joseph Cuvillier .... June 16, 1829 to Feb. 25, 1835.
Francis Schenig .... Feb. 26, 1835 to Dec. 9, 1836.
Raphael R. Triay .... Dec. 10, 1836 to May 22, 1843.
Antonio Pons .... May 22, 1843 to May 1, 1844.
Joseph Lucchesi .... May 1, 1844 to July 31, 1846.
Antonio Pons .... Oct. 26, 1846 to July 7, 1848.
Raphael R. Triay .... July 8, 1848 to Sept. 9, 1855.
Francis Scala .... Sept. 9, 1855 to Dec. 13, 1871.
Henry Fries .... Dec. 14, 1871 to Aug. 27, 1873.
Louis Schneider .... Sept. 2, 1873 to Oct. 1, 1880.
John Philip Sousa .... Oct. 1, 1880 to July 30, 1892.
Francisco Fanciulli ...... Nov. 1, 1892 to Oct. 31, 1897.
William H. Santelmann ... Mar. 3, 1898 to April 27, 1927.
Taylor Branson .... April 27, 1927 to

On July 4, 1801 President Jefferson reviewed the Marines, led by their historic Band, on the White House Grounds. This was the first time that a body of regular troops was ever reviewed by a President at his residence in Washington.

There is a false tradition which claims that the origin of the Marine Band lay in a group of kidnapped Italians. This tale has, in a small degree, withheld from the Marine Band a fair share of its glory as an American musical organization. "The music of a nation expresses its soul"; it "interprets its history, its religion, its patriotism, and its social customs, as do few single mediums." In America the Marine Band has most aptly illustrated this. And there is no American musical organization that has achieved more in this direction than our Marine Band. There is probably no organization that has exercised a more potent Americanizing influence than this Band. Let it be said right here that the foundation of the Marine Band is American and not transplanted Italian, as the false tradition has it. It is an American growth in root as well as in branch.

The Band often played in the Hall of Congress on Sundays, where their "glittering instruments and brilliant scarlet uniforms" made "a dazzling appearance." We read that on February 10, 1804, the "Marines attended in the gallery. After the services, they performed *Denmark*. The music was excellent. It was said they had only two days to learn the tune."

Thomas Jefferson, "the God-Father" of the Marine Band, called for its presence frequently during his two administrations. It played for James Madison when he became President on March 4, 1809, and on the evening of that date, at Long's Hotel, its stirring strains ushered in the First Inaugural Ball ever held. The ball opened at 7:00 o'clock when Thomas Jefferson entered, the Marine Band playing *Jefferson's March*. As President Madison, with "Sweet Dolly" on his arm, entered, the Band struck up *Madison's March*. *The Band* has been a familiar sight at practically every Inaugural Ball held since.

During the Second War with Great Britain the Marine Bandsmen not only helped to maintain national morale in the Capital with their martial music but some fought at the Battle of Bladensburg while others assisted in saving the early records of the Corps when the British burned the city.

The Band was unusually prominent during the Administrations of James Monroe and John Quincy Adams. It played at the White House several times for Lafayette, in 1824, and the following year, and accompanied the "Nation's Guest" to Mount Vernon and Yorktown. On September 6, 1825 (the birthday of Lafayette), President Adams rose and proposed the first toast ever drunk at a dinner in the President's House —"The Twenty-Second of February and the Sixth of September." The toast was drunk standing, to *The Marseillaise*, by the Marine Band, which also played an appropriate air to Lafayette's response—"The Fourth of July, the birthday of liberty in both hemispheres."

When Brigadier General Archibald Henderson, the Commandant of the Corps, received Lafayette at his residence, located at the Marine Barracks, Washington, the Marine Band rendered appropriate honors.

All Commandants have taken a special pride and interest in the Band, and have helped to foster its growth. None has been more active in the promotion of its welfare than Major General Ben H. Fuller, the present Commandant, who is keenly alive to its influence in helping to build up and sustain the finest traditions of American music. His residence is close to the Band's headquarters.

Around this old mansion, which is the traditional home of Marine Corps Commandants, some of the most stirring events in our country's history have occurred. It has been more than a century and a quarter since the first crudely-molded bricks were used to build it.

When the British burned Washington in 1814, the old house resisted the flames, and it is probably the oldest official residence in the capital. But the structure was not yielded without a struggle; the original doors and floors showed holes and scars made by British bayonets, and the old walls and staircase carried visible signs of bloodshed. Its capacious cellars once contained the treasure chest of the Marines, a strong box which held the entire funds for the annual pay, equipment and subsistence of the Corps.

Its historic walls have echoed to the music of the Band more often than has any other building in the country. The building is within a stone's throw of the Band headquarters, and in the shadow of its facade members of the Band or their predecessors have gathered for more than a hundred years to play martial music for marching Marines.

Often did the Band play for President Jackson his favorite air—*Auld Lang Syne*—and it also played in the presence of Jackson's fourteen-hundred pound "Mammoth Cheese" in 1829, as in 1802 it had for the seven-hundred-and-fifty pound "Great Cheese" of President Jefferson.

It played for President Polk and the Nation throughout the Mexican War and buoyed national spirit, while it also assisted in recruiting.

The Band had a very beneficial effect on public morale during the War of the Confederacy. President Lincoln insisted that it continue its out-door concerts and frequently called upon it to play at the White House. It also was present when Abraham Lincoln made his historic Gettysburg speech.

Abraham Lincoln and Andrew Johnson were sworn into office on March 4, 1865. Immediately after the conclusion of the address the Marine Band played "the National Air, *God Save Our President*," the music of which had been specially arranged for the Band. What

H. H. FLOREA, DRUM MAJOR

a remarkable coincidence that such a prayer should be carried to high heaven one month and ten days before he was stricken down by an assassin!

Shortly after he assumed office President Johnson reviewed General Hancock's Veteran Corps, prior to its disbandment. Being short on music, General Hancock borrowed the Marine Band for the occasion. It marched about two miles at the head of the column, formed in front of the President, and played while the entire Corps passed. General Hancock was so pleased that he shook hands with the Leader of the Band and invited the Bandsmen to have luncheon with the President of the United States at two long tables prepared under canvas.

The Band played at the first egg-rolling on the White House grounds and for the first White House children's party when Andrew Johnson was President.

It has played at all the important weddings in the White House, including those of Nellie Grant and Alice Roosevelt.

In its annual concert tours it has visited practically every State in the Union. The Band never has toured abroad but the World has come to America to hear it play. Thousands of prominent diplomats and other noted foreigners have heard it. When President Buchanan entertained the Prince of Wales (Edward VII) for a week at the White House, the Band virtually lived at the President's.

Not only on gala days has the Band performed for the President "and his Lady," but also on days of national bereavement. The Band led the two-mile-long funeral procession that mourned for William Henry Harrison and General Henderson with nine Marines guarded his body to North Bend. The Band played the funeral dirge for Zachary Taylor, for Abraham Lincoln, and accompanied the body of James A. Garfield to Cleveland. At the funeral of William Mc Kinley the Band played the hymns that were always dear to his heart—*Lead Kindly Light* and *Nearer My God to Thee*. In life the Band played for Warren G. Harding his favorite air, *Perfect Day*, and in his death it played the hymn he liked above all others, *Lead Kindly Light*.

Every President of the United States, except George Washington, has heard the music of the Marine Band and all of them have encouraged its improvement. It is also quite probable that George Washington, after he retired as President heard the Marine Band play at some time in Philadelphia. John Adams was the first President who heard the

Band play at the White House; President Jefferson was its sponsor and greatest friend; President Van Buren instituted the formal out-door concerts at the Capital Grounds, and President Tyler those at the White House Grounds; President Pierce in 1856 approved legislation according the Band extra emolument for playing on the grounds of the President and the Capital (after it had so played gratuitously for over eighteen years).

Finally Colonel John Harris, Commandant of the Marine Corps, recommended to Secretary of the Navy Gideon Welles, that Congress be requested to legislatively accord the Band the full official status that it deserved and to give it a statutory strength of one Principal Musician at a monthly salary of $90; seven first-class musicians at $34; eight second-class musicians at $21; and fifteen third-class musicians at $17 per month. The Drum Major was to be retained but the old grade of Fife Major was not asked for. Secretary Welles approved of the modest request of Colonel Harris and with the further approval of President Lincoln the matter was placed before Congress. That legislative body recognizing the importance of improving a public musical organization that played for all the official functions at the seat of government, including those at the White House, that furnished public out-door concerts, and attended national and international affairs in general, passed a bill that, on July 25, 1861, was approved by Abraham Lincoln. This act marked the recognition by law of the first band in the United States military service. The act expressly provided for "one Drum Major, one Principal Musician," "thirty Musicians for the Band, sixty drummers" and "thirty fifers." The Principal Musician received the informal title of "Leader," and the Drum Major was assigned the usual duties pertaining to such an office.

The status of the Band continued the same until 1899. In that year Colonel Commandant Charles Heywood earnestly recommended legislation that would increase the strength of the Band from thirty to sixty and add to the pay. Congress responded most generously and on March 3, 1899 President William Mc Kinley signed an Act of Congress that doubled the strength of the Band, gave the Band a Leader and a Second Leader. The exact wording of this law is as follows: "That the Band of the United States Marine Corps shall consist of one Leader, with the pay and allowances of a First Lieutenant; one Second Leader, whose pay shall be

THE UNITED STATES MARINE BAND ORCHESTRA

seventy-five dollars per month, and who shall have the allowances of a Sergeant-Major; thirty first-class musicians, whose pay shall be sixty dollars per month; and thirty second-class musicians whose pay shall be fifty dollars per month and the allowances of a Sergeant; such musicians of the Band to have no increased pay for length of service." William H. Santelmann was the first to occupy the office of Leader.

As members of the Band were permitted to accept engagements for private remuneration when such work did not interfere with their official duty, the Marine Band under this legislation afforded musicians an excellent opportunity and much fine material was added to its personnel.

The reorganization under this Act gave its Leader, William H. Santelmann, the opportunity of making it a first-class musical organization in every respect, and the development of the Band was exceedingly rapid.

The Band was further increased in 1916 during the administration of Major General Commandant George Barnett. In his recommendation to Secretary of the Navy, Josephus Daniels, which was passed by him to Congress, General Barnett, provided for a reclassification of the personnel of the Band, and for a substantial increase in pay. This recommendation was favorably received by Congress and on the 29th of August of that year President Woodrow Wilson by his signature made a law which established the strength of the Band at 65 Musicians and provided that the Leader should have the pay and allowances of a Captain in the Marine Corps. This legislation reads as follows:

"The Band of the United States Marine Corps shall consist of one Leader, whose pay and allowances shall be those of a Captain in the Marine Corps; one Second Leader, whose pay shall be $150 per month and who shall have the allowances of a sergeant-major; ten principal musicians, whose pay shall be $125 per month; twenty-five first-class musicians, whose pay shall be $100 per month; twenty second-class musicians, whose pay shall be $85 per month; and ten third-class musicians, whose pay shall be $70 per month; such musicians of the Band to have the allowances of a sergeant and to have no increase in the rates of pay on account of length of service."

Subsequent legislation, enacted on March 4, 1925, placed a new valuation on the worth of the Band and its pay was again increased substantially. It was just another acknowledgement by Congress that the Bandsmen were entitled to receive adequate remuneration and awards for their excellent services.

"That the Band of the United States Marine Corps shall consist of one Leader whose pay and allowances shall be those of a Captain in the Marine Corps; one Second Leader whose pay shall be $200 per month and who shall have the allowances of a sergeant-major; ten principal musicians whose pay shall be $150 per month; twenty-five first-class musicians whose pay shall be $125 per month; twenty second-class musicians whose pay shall be $100 per month; and ten third-class musicians whose pay shall be $85 per month; such musicians of the Band to have the allowances of a sergeant: *Provided*, That the Second Leader and musicians of the Band shall receive the same increases for length of service and the same enlistment allowance or gratuity for re-enlisting as is now or may hereafter be provided for other enlisted men of the Marine Corps: *Provided further*, That the pay authorized herein for the Second Leader and the musicians of the Band shall be effective from July 1, 1922, and shall apply in computing the pay of former members of the Band now on the retired list and who have been retired since June 30, 1922: *Provided further*, That in the event of promotion of the Second Leader, or a musician of the Band to leader of the Band, all service as such Second Leader, or as such musician of the Band, or both, shall be counted in computing longevity increase in pay: *And provided further*, That hereafter during concert tours approved by the President, members of the Marine Band shall suffer no loss of allowances."

The legislation set forth in this little history has not described two interesting features which should be understood by those who join this most historic musical organization. The first of these is that after a certain length of service a member of the Marine Band is entitled to retirement with sufficient remuneration for his support. The second is that concerning membership in the Marine Corps Reserve which is open to Marine Corps Bandsmen. In general, a Marine Bandsman, after having served a definite period (generally less than that provided for retirement) has the privilege of entering the Reserve at a proportion of his active service remuneration. Both of these interesting features require too much space to describe in a brief history like this but the details of them can be ascertained from Headquarters of the Corps, the Marine Band, or the nearest recruiting station.

Prior to March 3, 1899, the Marine Band was a magnificent organization with a history interwoven with that of the Presidents and the White House. Its Leaders were splendid musicians and many of them composers. In 1813 Leader Ashworth wrote a book on military music which was adopted by the Army, Navy and the Militia. Meritorious works were prepared by other Leaders. Led by John Philip Sousa, the famous "March King," the Band rose to heights never before reached by an American Military band.

The present leader, Taylor Branson, is a composer of merit, and has written a series of lively marches which he has dedicated to the Marine Corps in grateful appreciation of the opportunities afforded for advancement. Some of these marches are: *"Tell It to the Marines," "Marines of Belleau Woods," "The President's Own,"* and *"Eagle, Globe and Anchor."*

Presidents Hayes, Garfield, Arthur, Cleveland and Harrison not only very frequently expressed their high admiration of the performances of the Marine Band at the White House but were warm personal friends of John Philip Sousa. The incidents occurring at the White House described by Sousa in his charmingly written books and articles form an intimate part of the White House history.

While as early as 1801 it was accepted as the National Band and as the Band of the President and while it gradually added to its fame throughout the long years of our Nation's history, nevertheless it was not until 1899 that Congress afforded it an opportunity to reach its full development as a military band and as a symphonic organization. When, in that year, the Band was increased from thirty to sixty members, Mr. Santelmann thought it an appropriate time to organize a symphony orchestra within the band. With this end in view he required that every member of the Band double on a string instrument unless he be a soloist. Being himself a violinist of note and thoroughly experienced in symphony work he was very successful in this new venture. Mr. Santelmann after about four years of intelligent preparation declared in 1902, that the orchestra was ready for use at the White House and since that year the Marine Band has played there at all its indoor functions. as a symphony orchestra.

It has taken thirty-five years to gradually evolve the Marine Band from a remarkable military Band of wind instruments to its present status. It has taken unusual patience, endurance, and ability on the part of its Leaders to bring this result about.

An example of the Marine Band's versatility was exhibited on March 3, 1924 in Washington, D. C., when the Twenty-Fifth Anniversary of its Reorganization was observed by a Grand Concert. The Marine Band appeared in the First Part as a symphony Orchestra and in the Second Part as a Military Band. A distinguished audience was present on this occasion to hear a pleasing and satisfying completion of both parts of the concert. President Calvin Coolidge was regretfully absent but sent Mr. Santelmann an appreciative letter, accompanied with a huge basket of beautiful flowers.

During over a quarter of a century as Leader of the Marine Band, Mr. Santelmann led it in many important engagements of national and international importance. He was a composer of notable talent and ability. The band, under Mr. Santelmann, played for Presidents McKinley, Roosevelt, Taft, Wilson, Harding and Coolidge. Under his direction the Band furnished music on many occasions when visiting royalties and other high dignitaries were present and at ceremonies of great historic importance.

In April, 1927, after nearly thirty years of leadership, Mr. Santelmann placed the baton of leadership in the capable hands of Taylor Branson, the present leader.

Mr. Branson was born in Washington, July 31, 1881, and was educated in the public schools of that city. Like Sousa, who was an apprentice in the Marine Band in the early seventies, he enlisted in the band in 1898, just before the close of the Spanish-American War. He progressed through the various stages to second leader. Since 1922 he has carried the greater part of the exacting duties of the Band. He was solo violinist of the Marine Band Orchestra for more than twenty-five years.

Taylor Branson began the study of the violin when a boy under Mr. Santelmann, who was then a member of the Band, later taking lessons from Herman Rakeman, a well-known violinist. He studied the clarinet with Andrea Coda, solo clarinetist with the Band when Louis Schneider was the bandmaster, and composition with Arthur Tregina, former principal musician with the Band.

When radio broadcasting was in its infancy, Mr. Branson became identified to the radio fans throughout the country as the leader of the orchestra of the Marine Band that was broadcasting through the naval air station at Anacostia, D. C. The Marine Band is probably the pioneer in the broadcasting of large musical organizations.

Like John Philip Sousa who was elected to membership in the Gridiron Club of Washington in 1889 while serving as leader of the United States Marine Band, Taylor Branson is also a member of that world famous organization of newspaper correspondents and has been the director of the Gridiron Club Orchestra for more than a quarter of a century.

Mr. Branson is now carrying on the traditions of the Band, not only as a noteworthy leader, but also as one whose whole life, since early boyhood, has been interwoven in the accomplishments and the spirit of the organization he leads.

There are certain commands of the Marine Corps which have post or regimental bands authorized by the Major General Commandant. There is always a need for qualified musicians for these bands which are allowed specialists ratings. Those men who are rated specialists receive extra compensation.